Healthy Refreshing Salad
Recipes for Any Time

by *Maria Bertoli*

Healthy Refreshing Salad
Recipes for Any Time

Copyright: Published in the United States
by A New Horizon LLC / © Maria Bertoli

Published April 2014

All rights reserved. No part of this publication may be reproduced, stored in retrieval system, copied in any form or by any means, electronic, mechanical, photocopying, recording or otherwise transmitted without written permission from the publisher. Please do not participate in or encourage piracy of this material in any way. You must not circulate this book in any format. Maria Bertoli does not control or direct users' actions and is not responsible for the information or content shared, harm and/or actions of the book readers.

In accordance with the U.S. Copyright Act of 1976, the scanning, uploading and electronic sharing of any part of this book without the permission of the publisher constitute unlawful piracy and theft of the author's intellectual property. If you would like to use material from the book (other than just simply for reviewing the book), prior permission must be obtained by contacting the author at Maria@YourCenterforRecipes.com
Thank you for your support of the author's rights.

No book can replace the expertise and medical advice of a trusted physician. Please be certain to consult your doctor before making any decisions that affect your health or extreme changes to your diet, particularly if you suffer from any medical condition or have any symptom that may require treatment.

DISCLAIMER AND/OR LEGAL NOTICES:
The information presented herein represents the view of the author as of the date of publication. Because of the rate with which conditions change, the author reserves the right to alter and update his opinion based on the new conditions. This book is for informational purposes only. While every attempt has been made to verify the information provided in this book, neither the author nor his affiliates/partners assume any responsibility for errors, inaccuracies or omissions. Any slights of people or organizations are unintentional. If advice concerning legal or related matters is needed, the services of a fully qualified professional should be sought.

ISBN: 1941943020
ISBN-13: 9781941943021

Curb Your Hunger with a Cold, Crunchy Salad

Once summer comes, salads, smoothies, and icy drinks are your best friend. Cold salads and refreshments will not only cool down your body, but will also give you a ton of vitamins, minerals, and good-for-you nutrients to help endure the summer heat.

Eating fresh salad on a daily basis is a very easy habit that will allow you to include several servings of fruit and veggies into your diet. Although cooked vegetables have a lot of health benefits, they are bound to lose some of their vitamins and nutrients in the cooking process. Try to consume fresh veggies more often than not and soon you'll start enjoying all the amazing benefits: your sleeping habits will improve, your skin and eyes will shine, your digestive tract will calm down and you won't suffer from bloating, and you'll feel more and more energetic with each passing day.

There are two main mistakes that people tend to make when eating a salad. They will either make it very small and scarce in ingredients, or they will go overboard on heavy toppings and dressings that are high in calories and fat. The point of a salad is to completely satisfy your hunger without overloading your body with calories and fat.

A good start for any salad recipe is to fill it up with tons of leafy green veggies, like butter lettuce, iceberg, kale, spinach, romaine, arugula, or better yet, a combination of several salad greens. Follow up with a lot of juicy veggies, such as tomatoes, cucumbers, bell peppers, onions, carrots, and broccoli. Add some lean protein, like lean chicken breast, lean turkey breast, organic dairy, seafood, or legumes. Healthy salad dressings include olive oil, apple cider vinegar, Greek yogurt, lemon juice, balsamic vinegar, and even rich and cream avocados. You can also spice up your salad with berries or tropical fruits. Stay away from dressings that contain mayo or sour cream, and skip the croutons whenever you can.

I think you will really like our incredible crunchy salad recipes, that we've already divided into four categories: vegetarian salads, lean chicken and turkey salads, light and creamy pasta salads (that are great to make ahead and keep in the fridge for several days), and appetizing seafood salads. Some ingredients may be unusual, but if you try them, you may find yourself eating them much more often! Enjoy the upcoming hot weather days with these amazing salads that will satisfy even the pickiest eaters out there.

CONTENTS

Curb Your Hunger with a Cold, Crunchy Salad......iii

Simple Greek Salad 2

Red Cabbage and Walnut Coleslaw 4

Simple Mixed Green Salad.. 6

Fresh Israeli Salad 8

Roasted Red Pepper and Goat Cheese Salad.......... 10

Refreshing Tzatziki Dip 12

Warm Cauliflower Salad 14

Blood Orange and Avocado Salad 16

Strawberry and Spinach Salad................................ 18

Burrata Caprese Salad 20

Grilled Veggie Salad 22

Fresh Corn Salad 24

BLT Turkey Salad 28

Chicken and Chickpea Salad 30

Chicken, Feta, and Spinach Salad 32

Turkey, Mango, and Mint Salad............................. 34

Turkey Salad with Radish and Grape 36

Chicken Parmesan Salad 38

Curried Chicken Cauliflower Salad........................ 40

Skinny Waldorf Salad with Turkey 42

Summer Squash Pasta Salad................................... 46

Feta and Cherry Tomatoes Pasta Salad 48

Cold Soba Noodles with Peppers and Scallions 50

Three Bean Pasta Salad 52

Cucumber Chicken Orzo with Lemon and Mint 54

Brussels Sprout and Goat Cheese Couscous 56

Pepperoni Pasta Salad with Pesto 58

Creamy Eggplant and Mushroom Pasta Salad 60

Crab Salad with Eggs and Romaine 64

Apple and Jicama Slaw with Shrimp 66

Corn and Olive Tuna Pasta Salad 68

Salmon, Arugula, and Orange Salad 70

Shrimp and Black Bean Ceviche 72

Avocado and Cucumber Prawn Salad 74

Conclusion 77

Vegetarian Salads

Simple Greek Salad

Prep time: 10 minutes   Calories: 414   Serves: 2

This tasty Greek salad combines all the healthy flavors from the Mediterranean. It is packed with fresh veggies, creamy feta cheese, and healthy fats.

Ingredients

3 large tomatoes
2 English cucumbers
1 red onion
4 oz. feta cheese
10 Kalamata olives
2 tablespoons olive oil
juice from one lemon
dry oregano
salt and pepper

Method

1. Cut the tomatoes and cucumbers into bite-sized pieces. Slice the red onion.
2. Add the chopped veggies in a large salad bowl and season them with salt and pepper to taste.
3. Add two tablespoons olive oil and the juice from one lemon. Toss everything together.
4. Add the black olives to the salad and crumble the feta cheese right over the top.
5. Add a pinch of dry oregano and enjoy.

Tip: If you want your Greek salad to be on the sweet side use some juicy cherry tomatoes and red bell pepper.

Nutritional Information (per serving)

Calories: 414
Fat Total: 29.5g
Fat Saturated: 10.9g
Carbohydrates: 30.5g
Protein: 12.8g
Dietary Fiber: 7g

Red Cabbage and Walnut Coleslaw

Prep time: 10 minutes   Calories: 333   Serves: 2

Crunchy red cabbage, sweet and tart Gala apples, and buttery walnuts… This coleslaw is a true gourmet meal.

Ingredients

½ small head of red cabbage
1 Gala apple
2 carrots
4 scallions
small handful parsley
¼ cup walnuts
1 tablespoon olive oil
1 tablespoon packed brown sugar
1 tablespoon balsamic vinegar
juice of one lemon
salt and pepper

Method

1. Thinly slice the red cabbage and the onions.
2. Shred the carrots and the Gala apple.
3. Whisk the olive oil, balsamic vinegar, lemon juice, and brown sugar in a small bowl.
4. Mince the handful of parsley and coarsely chop the walnuts.
5. Combine all the salad ingredients in a large bowl and season them with salt and pepper to taste.
6. Pour the light dressing over the coleslaw and mix everything together. Enjoy.

Tip: If you don't like your coleslaw to be as sweet, use Granny Smith apples and skip the brown sugar.

Nutritional Information (per serving)

Calories: 333
Fat Total: 17.1g
Fat Saturated: 1.6g
Carbohydrates: 43g
Protein: 9g
Dietary Fiber: 10.5g

Simple Mixed Green Salad

Prep time: 10 minutes   Calories: 331   Serves: 2

We all want to enjoy amazing complex meals, but sometimes you just need something very clean and simple like this basic mixed green salad.

Ingredients

1 cup butter lettuce
1 cup baby spinach
1 cup arugula
2 tablespoons olive oil
1 tablespoon Dijon mustard
1 tablespoon apple cider vinegar
1 tablespoon honey
2 garlic cloves, crushed
¼ cup pecans, coarsely chopped
small handful dry cranberries
salt and pepper

Method

1. Loosely chop all the salad greens.
2. Whisk together the olive oil, Dijon mustard, apple cider vinegar, honey, and garlic for a simple vinaigrette.
3. Mix together the salad greens, chopped pecans, and cranberries in a large salad bowl. Season with salt and pepper to taste.
4. Drizzle with the simple dressing and toss everything together. Enjoy.

Tip: Every single salad green will work for this simple salad, so just use what you already have on hand.

Nutritional Information (per serving)

Calories: 331
Fat Total: 30.2g
Fat Saturated: 3.4g
Carbohydrates: 16.6g
Protein: 3.8g
Dietary Fiber: 3.9g

Fresh Israeli Salad

Prep time: 10 minutes   Calories: 155   Serves: 2

This classic Middle Eastern salad is the perfect choice for those unbearable summer afternoons, when the heat curbs your appetite, but you still want something flavorful to stop you from dehydrating.

Ingredients

2 small English cucumbers
2 ripe tomatoes
1 green bell pepper
2 scallions
1 tablespoon olive oil
2 tablespoons lemon juice
2 tablespoons minced parsley
salt and pepper

Method

1. Chop the cucumbers and the tomatoes as thinly as you possibly can.
2. Deseed the green bell pepper and chop it very thinly. Mince the scallions.
3. Whisk in the olive oil with the lemon juice and some salt and pepper.
4. Combine all the veggies in a salad bowl and pour over the light olive oil and lemon juice vinaigrette.
5. Sprinkle with minced parsley. Enjoy.

Tip: The art behind a great Israeli salad is in the chopping. Take the time to finely chop all your ingredients and enjoy this very delicate and refreshing salad.

Nutritional Information (per serving)

Calories: 155
Fat Total: 8.2g
Fat Saturated: 1.2g
Carbohydrates: 20.8g
Protein: 3.8g
Dietary Fiber: .4.9g

Roasted Red Pepper and Goat Cheese Salad

Prep time: 15 minutes   Cooking time: 40 minutes
Calories: 213   Serves: 4

Roasted red peppers are sweet, tender, and juicy. Here we'll combine them with creamy goat cheese and buttery walnuts.

Ingredients

8 red bell peppers
3 oz. goat cheese
¼ cup walnuts, coarsely chopped
1 tablespoon olive oil
1 tablespoon balsamic vinegar
2 tablespoons French parsley, minced
salt and pepper

Method

1. Preheat your oven to 400 degrees.
2. Line a large baking sheet with a piece of aluminum foil. Arrange the red peppers on the baking sheet making sure to leave some space between them.
3. Roast the pepper for 40 minutes flipping them once during the cooking process.
4. Take the peppers out of the oven and place them in a plastic bag while they are still steaming hot. After 5-10 minutes, take them out of the plastic bag and peel them.
5. Cut the roasted peppers into long strips and add them to a salad bowl.
6. Add the olive oil, balsamic vinegar, and the parsley to the peppers. Season them with salt and pepper. Mix until well combined.

7. Crumble the goat cheese over the peppers and top them with the chopped walnuts. Enjoy.

Tip: Roasted peppers should be a staple in your pantry, so stock up on jarred roasted pepper for those times when you need a quick bite.

Nutritional Information (per serving)

Calories: 213
Fat Total: 16g
Fat Saturated: 6g
Carbohydrates: 10.2g
Protein: 9.7g
Dietary Fiber: 2.3g

Refreshing Tzatziki Dip

Prep time: 10 minutes   Calories: 339   Serves: 4

This creamy salad is very tasty and refreshing, yet incredibly simple to make. The longer it stays in the fridge, the better it will taste, so make a big batch and enjoy it all week long.

Ingredients

3 English cucumbers
2 cups nonfat Greek yogurt
2 garlic cloves
1 tablespoon olive oil
1 teaspoon garlic powder
2 tablespoons lemon juice
¼ cup walnuts
dry dill
salt and pepper

Method

1. Grate the cucumbers or just chop them into teeny-tiny pieces.
2. Crush the garlic and coarsely chop the walnuts.
3. Mix the cucumbers with the Greek yogurt until combined.
4. Add the remaining ingredients and season with salt and pepper to taste. Enjoy.

Tip: The traditional recipe calls for fresh garlic, but if you're not a big fan of the raw garlic taste, just add the garlic powder and call it a day.

Nutritional Information (per serving)

Calories: 339
Fat Total: 17.2g
Fat Saturated: 1.9g
Carbohydrates: 28.4g
Protein: 24.9g
Dietary Fiber: .4.9g

Warm Cauliflower Salad

Prep time: 10 minutes   Cooking time: 20 minutes
Calories: 341   Serves: 2

Even in the summer heat there are days when you just feel as hungry as a bear. That's when this roasted cauliflower salad will come in handy.

Ingredients

4 cups kale, chopped
1 small head cauliflower, cut into florets
2 cups red cabbage, sliced
1 pink grapefruit, sliced
1 small red onion, sliced
1 tablespoon maple syrup
1 tablespoon balsamic vinegar
3 tablespoons olive oil
salt and pepper to taste

Method

1. Preheat your oven to 425 degrees.
2. Place the cauliflower florets in a baking sheet with one tablespoon olive oil and some salt and pepper. Bake for 20 minutes, or until tender.
3. In the meantime, mix together the kale, red cabbage, red onion, and pink grapefruit.
4. Whisk together the maple syrup, balsamic vinegar, olive oil, and salt and pepper for a delicious vinaigrette.
5. Top the salad with the hot cauliflower florets and the chopped pecans.
6. Pour over the dressing and enjoy.

Tip: If you don't like your salad to be as sweet, sub the maple syrup for some lemon juice, or just leave it out altogether.

Nutritional info (per serving)

Calories: 341
Fat Total: 20.4g
Fat Saturated: 2.4g
Carbohydrates: 37.5g
Protein: 8.3g
Dietary Fiber: 6.9g

Blood Orange and Avocado Salad

Prep time: 10 minutes   Calories: 358   Serves: 2

Smooth and creamy avocado, acidic blood orange, peppery watercress, and aromatic fennel: this salad packs it all in a gourmet lunch.

Ingredients

2 cups watercress
1 avocado
1 blood orange
1 small fennel bulb
1 tablespoon olive oil
1 tablespoon Dijon mustard
1 tablespoon apple cider vinegar
salt and pepper

Method

1. Peel and halve the avocado and cut it into bite-sized chunks.
2. Peel and segment the blood orange. Slice the fennel as thinly as you possibly can.
3. Mix together the olive oil, Dijon mustard, and apple cider vinegar. Season the dressing with salt and pepper.
4. Combine everything together in a medium salad bowl and toss with the vinaigrette. Enjoy.

Tip: Using a paring knife will make it easier to cut and segment the orange. Just cut through the membranes for uniformed, beautiful slices.

Nutritional info (per serving)

Calories: 358
Fat Total: 27.4g
Fat Saturated: 5.2g
Carbohydrates: 28.6g
Protein: 5.6g
Dietary Fiber: 13.2g

Strawberry and Spinach Salad

Prep time: 10 minutes   Calories: 342   Serves: 2

Adding different fruits to your summer salads not only makes them very delicious and complex in flavor, but also makes them nutritionally superior.

Ingredients

2 cups baby spinach
1 cup strawberries, sliced
3 oz. blue cheese
¼ cup almonds, coarsely chopped
1 tablespoon olive oil
1 tablespoon balsamic vinegar
1 tablespoon honey
2 tablespoons fresh mint, minced
salt and pepper

Method

1. Combine together olive oil, honey, balsamic vinegar, and minced mint in a light dressing. Season it with salt and pepper to taste.
2. Add the baby spinach and the sliced strawberries in a large salad bowl. Pour the dressing over and mix everything together.
3. Crumble the blue cheese over the salad and top with coarsely chopped almonds. Enjoy.

Tip: Gorgonzola cheese will work equally as well in this recipe.

Nutritional info (per serving)

Calories: 342
Fat Total: 25.5g
Fat Saturated: 9.4g
Carbohydrates: 18.9g
Protein: 13g
Dietary Fiber: 7.7g

Burrata Caprese Salad

Prep time: 10 minutes   Cooking time: 10 minutes
Calories: 206   Serves: 2

Italian Caprese salad is a very simple dish consisting of tangy mozzarella cheese and ripe tomatoes. We'll spice this salad with burrata cheese, which is made of mozzarella and cream, and an amazing balsamic reduction.

Ingredients

3 ripe tomatoes
3 oz. burrata cheese
¼ cup balsamic vinegar
big handful basil leaves
1 tablespoon olive oil
salt and pepper

Method

1. Add the balsamic vinegar to a small saucepan and bring it to a boil.
2. Simmer the balsamic for 10 minutes, or until it reduces in volume and thickens up a bit.
3. Slice the tomatoes and the burrata cheese.
4. Arrange the tomatoes and the burrata on a shallow plate, adding a basil leaf between each tomato and cheese slice.
5. Pour the balsamic reduction over the arranged tomatoes and cheese. Season with olive oil and salt and pepper to taste. Enjoy.

Tip: If you want your salad to be on the sweeter side, add one tablespoon of honey or maple syrup to the balsamic vinegar.

Nutritional info (per serving)

Calories: 206
Fat Total: 18g
Fat Saturated: 7.1g
Carbohydrates: 7.5g
Protein: 9.3g
Dietary Fiber: 2.2g

Grilled Veggie Salad

Prep time: 10 minutes   Cooking time: 10 minutes
Calories: 218   Serves: 4

Grilled veggies will come in handy for those days when you're fed up with fresh and crunchy salads. This salad is very sweet and moist and will blow your taste buds away.

Ingredients

2 zucchinis
1 eggplant
1 red onion
4 Portobello mushrooms
3 tablespoons olive oil
3 tablespoon balsamic vinegar
2 garlic cloves, crushed
small handful fresh basil
3 oz. parmesan cheese
salt and pepper

Method

1. Slice the veggies into thick slices and brush them with one tablespoon olive oil. Grill them for 10 minutes, turning them once halfway through.
2. Once the veggies are soft and have developed nice grill marks, chop them into bite-sized chunks.
3. Mix the remaining two tablespoons of olive oil with the balsamic vinegar and the crushed garlic.
4. Transfer the veggies in a large salad bowl and season them with salt and pepper. Mix in the balsamic vinaigrette and combine everything together.

5. Serve topped with fresh basil and shaved parmesan cheese. Enjoy.

Tip: Goat cheese or even feta would work beautifully with this salad.

Nutritional info (per serving)

Calories: 218
Fat Total: 15.5g
Fat Saturated: 4.6g
Carbohydrates: 13.8g
Protein: 9.4g
Dietary Fiber: 5.6g

Fresh Corn Salad

Prep time: 10 minutes   Calories: 218   Serves: 4

Nothing screams summer like fresh corn and juicy heirloom tomatoes. You can enjoy raw corn as long as it's in peak season and fresh.

Ingredients

2 cups fresh corn
4-5 heirloom tomatoes
½ avocado
2 tablespoons lemon juice
1 tablespoon olive oil
2 tablespoons parsley, minced
1 small red onion
salt and pepper

Method

1. Chop the heirloom tomatoes into bite-sized chunks. Finely dice the red onion.
2. Combine the veggies with the raw corn in a small salad bowl. Season with salt and pepper to taste.
3. Peel and chop the avocado and mash with a fork. Add the olive oil and the lemon juice and combine well together.
4. Add the avocado dressing to the corn salad and mix everything together. Finish with a sprinkle of fresh parsley. Enjoy.

Tip: The amount of heirloom tomatoes may vary depending on their size. If your tomatoes are bigger use just four, and if you have very small heirloom tomatoes, use up to eight.

Nutritional info (per serving)

Calories: 218
Fat Total: 20g
Fat Saturated: 4.7g
Carbohydrates: 27g
Protein: 7.7g
Dietary Fiber: 4.9g

Lean Chicken and Turkey Salads

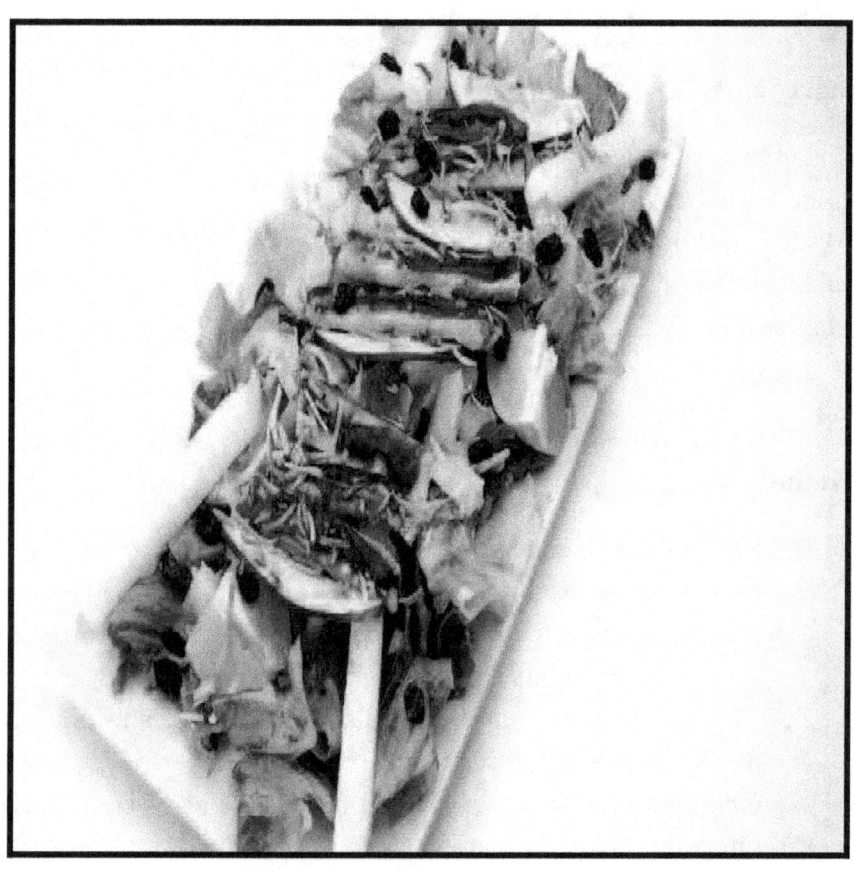

BLT Turkey Salad

Prep time: 5 minutes   Cooking time: 20 minutes
Calories: 260   Serves: 2

BLT may be the world's most famous sandwich, but it can be a little heavy for the hot summer days. We'll turn this popular sandwich into a crisp, amazing salad with turkey bacon.

Ingredients

1 head butter lettuce
4 ripe tomatoes
10 slices turkey bacon
1 tablespoon olive oil
2 tablespoons balsamic vinegar
fresh cilantro
salt and pepper

Method

1. Preheat your oven to 400 degrees.
2. Line a large baking sheet with aluminum foil. Place the sliced bacon on the baking sheet and cook it for 20 minutes, flipping it once halfway through.
3. Mix together the olive oil, balsamic vinegar, and cilantro. Season the dressing with some salt and pepper.
4. Chop the lettuce and cut the tomatoes into bite-sized pieces.
5. Once the turkey bacon has crisped up, slice it into medium-sized pieces.
6. Combine all salad ingredients in a bowl and pour over the balsamic dressing. Enjoy.

Tip: Don't go heavy handed with the salt, because you already have the salty bacon. Always taste and adjust your seasonings.

Nutritional info (per serving)

Calories: 260
Fat Total: 10.5g
Fat Saturated: 1.1g
Carbohydrates: 20.9g
Protein: 20.6g
Dietary Fiber: 7.5g

Chicken and Chickpea Salad

Prep time: 10 minutes   Calories: 244   Serves: 4

This is a hearty summer salad that comes packed with protein and crunchy radishes and celery.

Ingredients

2 chicken breasts, precooked
1 can chickpeas
2 cups butter lettuce
5 celery stalks
5 radishes
1 tablespoon olive oil
1 tablespoon white wine vinegar
2 tablespoons fresh dill, minced
salt and pepper

Method

1. Rinse and drain the canned chickpeas.
2. Cut the chicken breasts into bite-sized chunks. Slice and chop the radishes and the celery.
3. Mix the olive oil, white wine vinegar, and minced dill in a small bowl.
4. Combine all salad ingredients in a large bowl and season them with salt and pepper to taste.
5. Pour the dressing over your salad and enjoy.

Tip: Salads are a great way to use leftover chicken, or any leftover protein for that matter, so next time you're cooking chicken for dinner, double the amount and store the precooked meat in the fridge. You'll have ready-to-go salad protein for the rest of the week.

Nutritional info (per serving)

Calories: 244
Fat Total: 10.6g
Fat Saturated: 2.1g
Carbohydrates: 11g
Protein: 25.2g
Dietary Fiber: 3.2g

Chicken, Feta, and Spinach Salad

Prep time: 10 minutesCalories: 408Serves: 2

Spinach and feta is such a classic combination, but when combined with a lean chicken breast this combination turns into a complete healthy and tasty summer meal.

Ingredients

1 chicken breast, precooked
2 cups baby spinach
4 oz. feta cheese
1 red onion
2 carrots
1 tablespoon olive oil
1 tablespoon balsamic vinegar
salt and pepper

Method

1. Cut the chicken breast into bite-sized pieces.
2. Thinly slice the red onion and the carrots.
3. Combine the spinach, sliced veggies, and chopped chicken in a large salad bowl. Season them with olive oil, balsamic vinegar, and salt and pepper to taste.
4. Crumble the feta cheese right over the top. Enjoy.

Tip: The carrots and the onion provide a nice crunch to this salad, but you can leave them out if you prefer a smoother bite.

Nutritional info (per serving)

Calories: 408
Fat Total: 22.4g
Fat Saturated: 9.5g
Carbohydrates: 14.4g
Protein: 37.5g
Dietary Fiber: 3.6g

Turkey, Mango, and Mint Salad

Prep time: 10 minutes   Calories: 379   Serves: 2

This salad is incredibly fresh, light and bright. The sweet and juicy mangoes pair very well with the moist turkey, while the mint brightens up the dish.

Ingredients

1 cup turkey, precooked and chopped into bite-sized pieces
1 ripe mango
3 scallions
¼ cup pine nuts, toasted
2 tablespoons fresh mint, minced
1 tablespoon olive oil
2 tablespoons lemon juice
salt and pepper

Method

1. Peel and chop the mango into bite-sized chunks.
2. Thinly slice the scallions.
3. Combine turkey, mango, scallions, and pine nuts in a large salad bowl. Season with salt and pepper to taste.
4. Add olive oil, lemon juice, and minced mint. Mix everything together and enjoy.

Tip: Fresh basil would work equally as well, but you can also use a combination of the two or more herbs.

Nutritional info (per serving)

Calories: 379
Fat Total: 22.6g
Fat Saturated: 3.2g
Carbohydrates: 22.3g
Protein: 24.1g
Dietary Fiber: 3.5g

Turkey Salad with Radish and Grape

Prep time: 10 minutes   Calories: 308   Serves: 4

This salad comes bursting with summer flavors: crunchy radishes, sweet and juicy grapes, and creamy avocado. The turkey rounds up this salad with a protein punch.

Ingredients

2 cups turkey, precooked and shredded
1 avocado
1 cup red seedless grapes
4 radishes
1 red onion
1 English cucumber
1 tablespoon olive oil
2 tablespoons lime juice
salt and pepper

Method

1. Peel and chop the cucumber, avocado, and the radishes.
2. Slice the red onion and halve the red seedless grapes.
3. Combine the turkey, veggies, and seedless grapes in a large salad bowl. Season them with salt and pepper.
4. Add the olive oil and lime juice to the salad and mix everything together. Enjoy.

Tip: The avocado adds enough creaminess to this salad, but you can also add some crumbled feta or gorgonzola cheese. Keep in mind that adding cheese will increase the calorie and fat content of the dish.

Nutritional info (per serving)

Calories: 308
Fat Total: 17.0g
Fat Saturated: 3.8g
Carbohydrates: 18.6g
Protein: 22.5g
Dietary Fiber: 4.9g

Chicken Parmesan Salad

Prep time: 10 minutes   Cooking time: 10 minutes
Calories: 274   Serves: 4

This salad makes a spin on the classic Italian chicken parmesan. Sweet cherry tomatoes, tangy mozzarella cheese, peppery arugula, and moist chicken breast: this dish is a true family summer favorite.

Ingredients

2 chicken breasts, precooked
2 cups cherry tomatoes
1 cup baby arugula, packed
10 bocconcini balls (small mozzarella balls)
1 tablespoon olive oil
1 tablespoon balsamic vinegar
handful basil leaves
salt and pepper

Method

1. Heat the olive oil in a large non-stick skillet over medium high heat.
2. Cook the cherry tomatoes for 5-10 minutes, or until they burst. Season them with salt and pepper.
3. Add the arugula on the bottom of a shallow plate. Slice the chicken breasts and arrange them over the arugula.
4. Top each chicken slice with a few cherry tomatoes and some mozzarella balls.
5. Season the salad with olive oil, balsamic vinegar, and some salt and pepper.
6. Top with fresh basil leaves and enjoy.

Tip: If you can't find bocconcini balls you can use a standard mozzarella "ball" cut into bite-sized chunks.

Nutritional info (per serving)

Calories: 274
Fat Total: 15.8 g
Fat Saturated: 5.8g
Carbohydrates: 3.1g
Protein: 29.4g
Dietary Fiber: 1g

Curried Chicken Cauliflower Salad

Prep time: 10 minutes   Calories: 288   Serves: 4

This salad is fresh, crunchy, and very easy to make. It tastes great when served cold straight from the fridge, so make a big bunch and store up to three days.

Ingredients

2 chicken breasts, precooked
1 small head cauliflower
2 large carrots
2 scallions
1 tablespoon olive oil
1 tablespoon white wine vinegar
10 black olives, pitted
2 tablespoons fresh parsley, minced
1 teaspoon curry powder
salt and pepper

Method

1. Whisk together olive oil, white wine vinegar, curry powder, and fresh parsley for a spicy vinaigrette. Season it with salt and pepper and set aside.
2. Chop the chicken breasts into bite-sized chunks.
3. Cut the cauliflower into small florets. Peel and slice the carrots.
4. Thinly slice the scallions and add them to a large salad bowl along with the remaining veggies and cubed chicken. Slice the black olives and add them to the salad.
5. Pour over the curry dressing and combine everything together. Enjoy.

Tip: You can also grate the carrots if you don't like that many crunchy elements in your salad.

Nutritional info (per serving)

Calories: 288
Fat Total: 13.7g
Fat Saturated: 2.9g
Carbohydrates: 11g
Protein: 30.7g
Dietary Fiber: 4.3g

Skinny Waldorf Salad with Turkey

Prep time: 10 minutes   Calories: 313   Serves: 2

Traditional Waldorf salad is rich, creamy, and sweet, but for this recipe we'll make it a bit lighter and healthier.

Ingredients

1 cup turkey, precooked and cubed
1 Fiji apple
½ cup red seedless grapes
2 celery stalks
¼ cup walnuts, coarsely chopped
1/3 cup nonfat Greek yogurt
1 tablespoon white rice vinegar
salt and pepper

Method

1. Chop the Fiji apple into bite-sized chunks. Halve the seedless grapes.
2. Dice the celery stalks into pretty small pieces.
3. Whisk the white rice vinegar with the Greek yogurt until combined.
4. Add the turkey, apple, grapes, and celery to a medium salad bowl. Season with salt and pepper to taste.
5. Mix in the Greek yogurt until well combined and creamy.
6. Fold the chopped walnuts and enjoy.

Tip: Folding the walnuts just before the end will prevent them from getting soggy.

Nutritional info (per serving)

Calories: 313
Fat Total: 13.3g
Fat Saturated: 2.1g
Carbohydrates: 23.3g
Protein: 27.9g
Dietary Fiber: 4.1g

Light and Creamy Pasta Salads

Summer Squash Pasta Salad

Prep time: 15 minutes   Calories: 411 Serves: 6

Summer squash and Greek yogurt mousse over small macaroni pasta: this salad is so creamy; you won't be able to stop eating it.

Ingredients

1 yellow summer squash
1 zucchini
1 cup Greek yogurt
1 pound macaroni, precooked
1 tablespoon olive oil
big handful fresh parsley
salt and pepper

Method

1. Chop the summer squash and the zucchini into pretty large chunks.
2. Add the zucchini, summer squash, fresh parsley, and Greek yogurt to a food processor or a blender and pulse until smooth.
3. Season the summer squash dip with one tablespoon olive oil and some salt and pepper to taste.
4. Add the pasta to the squash mousse and combine well together. Enjoy.

Tip: You can refrigerate this pasta salad for 5-6 days, and the longer it cools before serving, the better it will taste.

Nutritional info (per serving)

Calories: 411
Fat Total: 6.3g
Fat Saturated: 2.6g
Carbohydrates: 64g
Protein: 24.1g
Dietary Fiber: 3.1g

(Yogurt might be hard to get in your area, but try and get your store manager to order it – it's worth it)

Feta and Cherry Tomatoes Pasta Salad

Prep time: 10 minutes   Calories: 245   Serves: 4

This pasta salad is a spin on a tomato and feta Greek salad. The starchy pasta goes well with the creamy cheese, and the veggies add some crunch and bright flavors.

Ingredients

½ pound whole wheat orecchiette pasta, precooked
5 oz. feta cheese
1 ½ cups cherry tomatoes
1 English cucumber
1 tablespoon olive oil
1 tablespoon apple cider vinegar
10 black olives, pitted
salt and pepper

Method

1. Chop the cucumber into bite-sized pieces and halve the cherry tomatoes.
2. Slice the black olives.
3. Add the cooked pasta in a large salad bowl and mix with the veggies and the sliced olives. Season with olive oil, apple cider vinegar, and salt and pepper to taste.
4. Crumble the feta cheese over the top and gently fold it in with the pasta and veggies. Enjoy.

Tip: Goat cheese could work equally as well with this pasta salad.

Nutritional info (per serving)

Calories: 245
Fat Total: 9.3g
Fat Saturated: 4g
Carbohydrates: 32.6g
Protein: 8.7g
Dietary Fiber: 4.3g

Cold Soba Noodles with Peppers and Scallions

Prep time: 10 minutes   Calories: 309   Serves: 6

This noodle pasta salad comes with a wide range of crunchy summer veggies and a spicy dressing full of Asian flavors.

Ingredients

1 pound soba noodles, precooked
1 red bell pepper
1 yellow bell pepper
1 green bell pepper
4 scallions
2 carrots
1 tablespoon sesame oil
1 tablespoon soy sauce
1 tablespoon lemon juice
1 tablespoon fresh ginger, crushed
salt and pepper

Method

1. Slice all your veggies into long, thin strips. You're trying to imitate the shape of the noodles with the veggies.
2. Whisk the sesame oil, soy sauce, lemon juice, and fresh ginger in a small bowl. Season your dressing with some salt and pepper.
3. Combine the soba noodles and the veggies in a large salad bowl. Pour the ginger and soy dressing over the pasta salad and mix until combined. Be careful not to break the soba noodles.
4. Season with salt and pepper to taste and enjoy.

Tip: You can also use rice noodles if that's what you have on hand.

Nutritional info (per serving)

Calories: 309
Fat Total: 3.1g
Fat Saturated: 0g
Carbohydrates: 63.6g
Protein: 12.1g
Dietary Fiber: 2.2g

Three Bean Pasta Salad

Prep time: 10 minutes   Calories: 403   Serves: 8

This bean pasta salad is so easy; you can literally assemble it over your kitchen sink. It's very hearty and packed with protein.

Ingredients

1 pound of precooked elbow pasta
1 can black beans
1 can red kidney beans
1 can cannellini beans
2 cups kale, packed
1 tablespoon olive oil
1 tablespoon red wine vinegar
2 garlic cloves, crushed
1 tablespoon Worcestershire sauce
salt and pepper

Method

1. Rinse and drain all the canned beans and transfer them to a large bowl.
2. Tear the kale using your hand and add it to the beans.
3. Whisk the olive oil, Worcestershire sauce, red wine vinegar, and crushed garlic in a small bowl.
4. Add the elbow pasta to the beans and kale. Combine everything together and season with salt and pepper to taste.
5. Pour the dressing over your salad and give it one final stir. Enjoy.

Tip: Any combination of beans will work for this salad, and you can also add fresh corn.

Nutritional info (per serving)

Calories: 403
Fat Total: 3.2g
Fat Saturated: 0g
Carbohydrates: 73.4g
Protein: 21.1g
Dietary Fiber: 14.5g

Cucumber Chicken Orzo with Lemon and Mint

Prep time: 10 minutes   Calories: 302   Serves: 4

This pasta salad is a true epiphany of summer. It has just the right amount of protein, carbs, and minerals for a well-rounded summer meal.

Ingredients

½ pound orzo, precooked
1 large chicken breast, precooked
2 cucumbers
4 tablespoons lemon juice
1 tablespoon olive oil
big handful fresh mint, minced
salt and pepper

Method

1. Add the orzo to a large bowl and season it with olive oil, lemon juice, fresh mint, and salt and pepper to taste.
2. Cut the cucumbers and the chicken breast into bite-sized chunks.
3. Combine all ingredients together and serve with one last kiss of fresh mint and a squeeze of lemon juice. Enjoy.

Tip: You can sub the cucumbers for steamed or grilled asparagus. This will give your salad a sweeter taste.

Nutritional info (per serving)

Calories: 302
Fat Total: 5.7g
Fat Saturated: 0.6g
Carbohydrates: 47.8g
Protein: 14.9g
Dietary Fiber: 2.9g

Brussels Sprout and Goat Cheese Couscous

Prep time: 10 minutes   Calories: 422   Serves: 4

Boiled Brussels sprouts have a not-so-appetizing smell and texture that a lot of people try to avoid. When eaten raw, they are crunchy, sweet, and very nutritious.

Ingredients

1 pound Brussels sprouts
1 cup couscous, precooked
4 oz. fresh goat cheese
¼ cup pistachios, coarsely chopped
1 tablespoon olive oil
2 tablespoons lemon juice
½ red onion
1/3 teaspoon cayenne pepper
salt and pepper

Method

1. Add the couscous in a large salad bowl and season it with olive oil, lemon juice, cayenne pepper, and salt and pepper to taste.
2. Cut the stems of the Brussels sprouts and start breaking up all the individual layers. Add them to the couscous.
3. Finely dice the red onion and transfer to the salad bowl. Mix everything together until well combined.
4. Sprinkle the goat cheese and the chopped pistachios right over the top. Fold gently and enjoy.

Tip: Walnuts or toasted pine nuts would work equally as well.

Nutritional info (per serving)

Calories: 302
Fat Total: 17.6g
Fat Saturated: 8.1g
Carbohydrates: 48.1g
Protein: 19.7g
Dietary Fiber: 7.5g

Pepperoni Pasta Salad with Pesto

Prep time: 10 minutes   Calories: 333   Serves: 4

This salad is perfect for all meat lovers that enjoy bold flavors. The rich pesto plays well with the smoky pepperoni.

Ingredients

½ pound whole wheat macaroni, precooked
3 oz. turkey pepperoni
4 tablespoons pesto
1 cup baby spinach
1 tablespoon lemon juice
½ cup frozen peas, defrosted
2 tablespoons cilantro, minced
salt and pepper

Method

1. Combine the pesto, lemon juice, cilantro, and salt and pepper in a small bowl.
2. Add the pasta, baby spinach, pepperoni, and peas to a large salad bowl.
3. Depending on how salty is your pepperoni; season it with salt and pepper. If your meat is very salty, just add freshly ground black pepper.
4. Pour the dressing over your salad and mix everything together. Enjoy.

Tip: The amount of pesto may vary depending on how creamy you like your pasta to be. Start with four tablespoons and then add more if you feel like that's not enough.

Nutritional info (per serving)

Calories: 333
Fat Total: 10.2g
Fat Saturated: 2.5g
Carbohydrates: 46.8g
Protein: 17.5g
Dietary Fiber: 6.3g

Creamy Eggplant and Mushroom Pasta Salad

Prep time: 10 minutes   Cooking time: 10 minutes
Calories: 341   Serves: 4

This pasta salad is the perfect summer meal to serve when you're trying to impress somebody. It's creamy, luscious, and full of flavor.

Ingredients

½ pound bowties, precooked
1 eggplant
1 pound button mushrooms
4 tablespoons Greek yogurt
2 tablespoons olive oil
1 garlic clove
2 oz. parmesan cheese
big handful fresh dill, minced
salt and pepper

Method

1. Slice the eggplant into fairly thick slices. Quarter the mushrooms.
2. Season the veggies with one tablespoon olive oil and a pinch of salt and pepper.
3. Grill the veggies for 5-10 minutes, or until they develop some color.
4. Add the bowties in a large salad bowl and combine with the grilled mushrooms.
5. Add the eggplant to a food processor with the Greek yogurt, garlic, and two tablespoons olive oil. Pulse until smooth and creamy.

6. Transfer the eggplant dip to the pasta with the mushrooms and mix everything together.
7. Finish the pasta salad with fresh dill and some shaved parmesan cheese. Enjoy.

Tip: If you don't like the bitter taste of the eggplant skin, grill it with the skin on, and then peel off the skin. If you remove the skin before you grill the eggplant, it will turn to mush.

Nutritional info (per serving)

Calories: 341
Fat Total: 14.9g
Fat Saturated: 6g
Carbohydrates: 23.3g
Protein: 30g
Dietary Fiber: 5.1g

Seafood Salads

Crab Salad with Eggs and Romaine

Prep time: 10 minutes   Calories: 341   Serves: 4

Crab and eggs is a match made in heaven. We'll keep this salad light by using nonfat Greek yogurt instead of heavy mayo.

Ingredients

1 can crabmeat
4 hard-boiled eggs
2 celery stalks
2 scallions
1 carrot
½ head romaine lettuce
4 tablespoons nonfat Greek yogurt
1 tablespoon lime juice
salt and pepper

Method

1. Dice the eggs and combine them with the crabmeat in a bowl.
2. Dice the celery, scallions, and carrot. Add them to the crab mixture.
3. Mix the veggies with the crab and eggs, and add the Greek yogurt, lime juice, and some salt and pepper to taste. Combine well together.
4. Serve over a bed of chopped romaine lettuce. Enjoy.

Tip: You can easily turn this recipe into deviled eggs and adapt it for a party.

Nutritional info (per serving)

Calories: 341
Fat Total: 4.8g
Fat Saturated: 1.5g
Carbohydrates: 21.4g
Protein: 29.1g
Dietary Fiber: 2.6g

Apple and Jicama Slaw with Shrimp

Prep time: 10 minutes Cooking time: 6 minutes
Calories: 278 Serves: 4

Shrimp is a great summer salad protein, and here we'll serve it with an apple and jicama tropical slaw.

Ingredients

10 oz. shrimp, peeled and deveined
1 small head cabbage
1 jicama
1 Gala apple
3 scallions
1 teaspoon + 1 tablespoon olive oil
2 tablespoons coconut milk
2 tablespoons pineapple juice
1 tablespoon apple cider vinegar
1 teaspoon brown sugar
salt and pepper

Method

1. Heat one teaspoon olive oil in a non-stick skillet over medium high heat. Cook shrimp for 3 minutes on each side.
2. Thinly cut the cabbage, scallions, apple, and jicama. Transfer to a large salad bowl and season with salt and pepper.
3. Mix together a tablespoon of olive oil, pineapple juice, coconut milk, apple cider vinegar, and brown sugar.
4. Pour the dressing over the slaw and mix well together. Top with the cooked shrimp and enjoy.

Tip: You can add more brown sugar or even honey if you want a sweeter slaw.

Nutritional info (per serving)

Calories: 278
Fat Total: 8.2g
Fat Saturated: 2.7g
Carbohydrates: 33g
Protein: 20.1g
Dietary Fiber: 13.5g

Corn and Olive Tuna Pasta Salad

Prep time: 10 minutes   Calories: 302   Serves: 4

Nothing beats a refreshing, bright, and creamy pasta salad to cool you off on a hot summer afternoon.

Ingredients

1 cup macaroni, precooked
1 can tuna
1 English cucumber
2 scallions
1/3 cup frozen corn, defrosted
10 green olives, pitted
½ cup Greek yogurt
2 tablespoons parsley, minced
1 tablespoon lime juice
salt and pepper

Method

1. Shred the cucumber and the scallions. Dice the green olives.
2. Rinse and drain the canned tuna and transfer to a large bowl.
3. Add the veggies, corn, parsley, lime juice, and Greek yogurt to the tuna. Mix everything together until well incorporated.
4. Season with salt and pepper to taste and enjoy.

Tip: You can one or two tablespoons of low-fat mayo if you feel like the Greek yogurt doesn't make it rich enough.

Nutritional info (per serving)

Calories: 302
Fat Total: 5.5g
Fat Saturated: 1.7g
Carbohydrates: 30.7g
Protein: 33.7g
Dietary Fiber: 3.2g

Salmon, Arugula, and Orange Salad

Prep time: 10 minutes   Calories: 215   Serves: 4

This salad is a very simple and delicious way to use up any leftover cooked salmon. The arugula gives the dish a nice kick and the orange brightens up the flavors.

Ingredients

2 salmon fillets, precooked
2 cups arugula
2 oranges
1 cup broccoli florets
1 red onion
1 tablespoon olive oil
1 tablespoon lemon juice
1 tablespoon lemon zest
salt and pepper

Method

1. Flake the salmon into small chunks and transfer to a large bowl.
2. Peel and slice the oranges and add to the flaked salmon.
3. Dice the onion and add it to the salad bowl along with the broccoli florets.
4. Whisk together the olive oil, lemon juice, lemon zest, and some salt and pepper to taste.
5. Pour the dressing over the salad and combine everything together. Enjoy.

Tip: Try not to over mix the salad because that will turn the salmon to mush. You want the fish to stay chunky.

Nutritional info (per serving)

Calories: 215
Fat Total: 9.3g
Fat Saturated: 1.3g
Carbohydrates: 15.6g
Protein: 19.3g
Dietary Fiber: 3.6g

Shrimp and Black Bean Ceviche

Prep time: 10 minutes Cooking time: 2 minutes
Calories: 404 Serves: 4

This ceviche is a fancy dish that will impress any guest that you have over for dinner. The lightness of the shrimp plays well with the hardiness of the black beans.

Ingredients

1 pound shrimp, peeled and deveined
1 can black beans
1 red onion
1 red bell pepper
1 cucumber
1 tablespoon olive oil
juice from 6 limes
juice from 2 lemons
2 tablespoons coconut milk
big handful cilantro, minced
salt and pepper

Method

1. Cook the shrimp in salted boiling water for two minutes. Remove from heat and drain well.
2. Chop the cucumber and the bell pepper into small cubes. Finely dice the onion.
3. Whisk the olive oil, coconut milk, lime juice, lemon juice, and minced cilantro in a large bowl. Season with salt and pepper to taste.
4. Add the shrimp, veggies, and rinsed beans to the bowl. Combine well together.
5. Serve in martini glasses and enjoy.

Tip: You can cut back on the lime juice and add some freshly squeezed orange juice if you feel like the lemony flavor is overpowering your ceviche.

Nutritional info (per serving)

Calories: 404
Fat Total: 8.4g
Fat Saturated: 3.1g
Carbohydrates: 45.7g
Protein: 37.9g
Dietary Fiber: 9.6g

Avocado and Cucumber Prawn Salad

Prep time: 10 minutes   Calories: 287   Serves: 4

This Thai inspired prawn salad comes with creamy avocado, crunchy cucumbers and tomatoes, and salty peanuts.

Ingredients

1 pound prawns, peeled and cooked
2 English cucumbers
2 cups cherry tomatoes
4 scallions
1 avocado
2 cups baby spinach
1 tablespoon lime juice
1 tablespoon rice vinegar
fresh mint
salt and pepper

Method

1. Chop the cucumbers into bite-sized chunks. Halve the cherry tomatoes.
2. Finely dice the scallions.
3. Add all veggies in a large salad bowl and season with salt and pepper.
4. Peel and mash the avocado with the lime juice, rice vinegar, and salt and pepper to taste.
5. Combine the avocado dressing with the veggies and mix well. Add the prawns and give it a one last stir.
6. Serve topped with fresh mint. Enjoy.

Tip: You can add fish sauce or chili oil for a more authentic Thai salad taste.

Nutritional info (per serving)

Calories: 287
Fat Total: 12.3g
Fat Saturated: 2.7g
Carbohydrates: 17g
Protein: 29.1g
Dietary Fiber: 5.9g

Conclusion

Thank you again for purchasing this book!

I hoped you enjoyed the recipes and get many years of use out of them in my book on **Healthy, Refreshing Salad Recipes for Any Time.**

Finally, if you enjoyed this book, please take the time to share your thoughts and write me an honest review about the book – I truly value your opinion and thoughts and I will incorporate them into my next book, which is already underway. **Please post your review on Amazon**. (just type the title - **Healthy, Refreshing Salad Recipes for Any Time** – in the Amazon URL or go directly to http://www.amazon.com/dp/B00K0R7Q1O and the page will come up to enter reviews). It'd be greatly appreciated. A kind review is always helpful and keeps me inspired.

Take care and Healthy, Happy Eating!!!

Maria Bertoli

Hello,

Maybe like you, I enjoy finding new recipes and creating my own recipes, especially when I can keep the prep time less than 15 or 20 minutes, unless it's a special meal I'm making.

However, I love spending time with my family a whole lot more, especially that special little fellow I'm holding in the picture. That's our grandson, Alex. He's our center of pride and joy, along with his father (our son), and his wife.

My husband (of 36+ years) and I are putting together our favorite recipes which take the minimum amount of prep time, but yield a delicious meal!!

We hope you enjoy each of our books in the Food Recipe Series. We'll be including everything from a Healthy 2 Week Meal Plan to the Ultimate Mouthwatering Pizzas and much, much more.

All our books and recipes can be found at www.YourCenterforRecipes.com. This will be a continually growing site as we add our recipes for all kinds of foods and our reader's special recipes that they would like to share. Please come and join us and think about sending in your favorite recipe. Who knows, you might find your recipe and name in one of our upcoming books!!

Feel free to contact me at Maria@YourCenterforRecipes.com.

Till then, take care and enjoy that healthy eating (as well as a little splurge once in a while – we all need that!!).

Maria Bertoli

Please, Check out Our Other Books at Their Amazon URLs

A 2 Week Healthy, Easy Meal Plan

http://www.amazon.com/ dp/B00JBNWYYC/

10 Mouthwatering DIY Pizza Recipes

http://www.amazon.com/dp/B00K2279ZU

Weight Loss on the Go with Tasty Detox Smoothie Recipes

http://www.amazon.com/ dp/B00L99M3LA

www.ingramcontent.com/pod-product-compliance
Lightning Source LLC
LaVergne TN
LVHW051849080426
835512LV00018B/3158